fast
thinking.
decision

C000259033

PEARSON EDUCATION LIMITED

Head Office:
Edinburgh Gate
Harlow CM20 2JE
Tel: +44 (0)1279 623623
Fax: +44 (0)1279 431059

London Office:
128 Long Acre
London WC2E 9AN
Tel: +44 (0)20 7447 2000
Fax: +44 (0)20 7240 5771
Website: www.business-minds.com

First published in Great Britain in 2001

© Pearson Education Limited 2001

The right of Ros Jay to be identified as Author
of this Work has been asserted by her in accordance
with the Copyright, Designs and Patents Act 1988.

ISBN 0 273 65306 7

British Library Cataloguing in Publication Data
A CIP catalogue record for this book can be obtained from the British Library

All rights reserved; no part of this publication may be reproduced, stored
in a retrieval system, or transmitted in any form or by any means, electronic,
mechanical, photocopying, recording, or otherwise without either the prior
written permission of the Publishers or a licence permitting restricted copying
in the United Kingdom issued by the Copyright Licensing Agency Ltd,
90 Tottenham Court Road, London W1P 0LP. This book may not be lent,
resold, hired out or otherwise disposed of by way of trade in any form
of binding or cover other than that in which it is published, without the
prior consent of the Publishers.

10 9 8 7 6 5 4 3 2 1

Typeset by Pantek Arts Ltd, Maidstone, Kent.
Printed and bound in Great Britain by Ashford Colour Press, Hampshire.

The Publishers' policy is to use paper manufactured from sustainable forests.

fast
thinking:
decision

▶ **gather the facts**

▶ **weigh up the options**

▶ **make the right choice**

by Ros Jay

contents

introduction

It's decision time. You've been putting it off through pressure of work, or simply because you've no idea what decision to make. But now it's crunch time. It has reached the point where not making a decision is worse than having to make it. People are yelling, problems are mounting, the pressure is piling up … and all because everything is waiting on your decision. But what should it be?

You're worried you'll make the wrong decision. You're worried you won't be able to make a decision at all. You're worried the yelling will get even louder. Well, you can stop worrying now. This book will guide you quickly and cleanly through the process, and before you know it the decision will be clear. Obvious, even. And once you've learnt the system this time, decisions will never seem so scary again.

As a manager, you may not have to make that many big decisions. But their importance is out of all proportion to the time they occupy: it is one of the most important parts of your job. The kind of decisions managers have to make can cover a massive range of possibilities. Here are just a few of them to give you a flavour of the kind of decision this book is about:

- which candidate to appoint following last week's selection interviews
- what to do about the bottleneck in the production line
- which supplier to sign with for the next year
- whether to give a big customer the extremely big discount they're demanding
- whether to put the entire marketing budget into one huge campaign next year, or whether to spend it on several smaller campaigns
- which product name to go with for the new range
- whether to stop providing company cars for employees who don't travel as part of the job.

They may not be earth-shattering decisions on a global scale, but they're a good deal more important than what time to take your coffee break. And, invariably, they affect other people. That's why they've all started yelling. They have decisions to make – whether large or small – which are hanging on your decision. And all that pressure just seems to make the whole thing worse.

Don't worry. This time tomorrow, they'll all have the decision they need (even if it isn't the one they want). In an ideal world you'd have given yourself longer to make this decision, but this isn't an ideal

It has reached the point where not making a decision is worse than having to make it

world. Anyway, now you know, you'll leave longer next time (won't you?). This book will fill you in on how to invest the extra time in future. Meantime, you want to get this decision made – and you need to be sure it's the right one. So you need:

 tips for pulling together the information you need fast

 shortcuts for avoiding any unnecessary work

 checklists to make sure you have all the essentials covered

… all put together clearly and simply. And short enough to read fast, of course.

And what if you've cut it even finer than I was allowing for? What if the decision has to be made by this afternoon? Well, don't panic. Anything's possible. At the back of the book you'll find a brief guide to making a decision in an evening. In fact, even if you've squeezed the decision into the final hour before the deadline, you can still manage it. The one-hour version at the end shows you how to pull out all the stops and work at the speed of life.

So relax. Take a deep breath, and go and get yourself a cup of coffee before you start. You're not just going to make the decision here, you're going to make the very best possible decision. After all, the wrong decision can be worse than no decision at all. So we're not only going to act fast, we're going to think smart too.

work at the speed of life

This book will take you swiftly and simply through the seven key steps of decision making:

1 The very first stage is to identify your objective. It may sound obvious, but it can go dramatically wrong if you don't think before you start, and be sure you're making the right decision.

2 Next, you need to decide to take the decision. I know it sounds pathetically obvious, but actually managers often go wrong by taking a decision that they should have passed on to someone else, or that should have been deferred.

3 Once you're clear about exactly what you're aiming to achieve, it's time to assemble all the facts you need. Without them, you cannot be sure of making the best decision.

4 I've already mentioned that your decision is bound to affect other people. This is why you must consult. It can take days or even weeks, but we're going to do it in a matter of hours, because that's all we've got.

5 You can't possibly decide what action to take until you know what the options are. So this next stage is all about identifying your options.

6 Here it comes: decision time. But once you've been through the earlier stages, you'll find it's nothing like as daunting as it looked from a distance. And we'll be looking at all sorts of tips and tools for helping you reach the right decision.

7 Once you've made the decision, it's no good keeping it to yourself. You have to communicate it to all those yelling people. And since it's your decision, you have to look after it and make sure it's followed through.

This book will take you swiftly and simply through the seven key steps of decision making

fast thinking gambles

This sounds easy. Shall we make all our decisions in 24 hours from now on? What's the point in spending any longer on them if we don't have to? Well, it can be done in 24 hours, but it really isn't the best way. Just because you're getting away with it this time, doesn't mean your luck can hold out for ever. There are reasons why you really need to leave longer for this kind of important decision if you possibly can.

- The most obvious gamble you take is that you may not come up with the best decision. If you follow the guidelines in this book you'll certainly avoid making bad decisions, but that isn't the same thing as making the best possible decision.

- One of the vital, and sometimes the most time-consuming, stages of the process is collecting all the facts. Sometimes certain key facts simply can't be found this fast. It might take a few days – perhaps the only person with the vital information is on holiday, or maybe you have to run tests to find out what outcome certain actions would have.

- You need to consult other people for the vast majority of decisions. This can take a while to organise, particularly if you want to talk to a group of employees or colleagues.
- Consultation has a psychological angle too: people like to feel involved. If they feel they are being consulted at the last minute, without time to prepare their response fully, they will be resentful whatever decision you finally arrive at. For controversial decisions this can be catastrophic.

Fast thinking will ensure that you reach a decision – and a good one at that – in minimal time. Right now, I imagine that's the most important thing. But if you want to make the best decision every time, and keep everyone else happy into the bargain, you'll need to leave yourself a little more time in future.

1 identify your objective

The most vital part of the whole process is the bit that comes right at the beginning. If you're even slightly adrift at the start, you could be way off course by the end of the thing – the decision itself. So setting your objective is not a waste of precious time (I'm sure that never crossed your mind); it's your means of navigating your way through the decision. Set your course correctly from the outset, and the whole journey will run more smoothly, and you'll arrive at the right destination.

And you do all this by identifying your objective. Suppose the problem that you are trying to resolve is that there is a bottleneck in the production department. It's creating frustrations and slowing down production to a point where you can't fulfil orders on time. You have to decide what to do about it. But you'll run into difficulties early on if your objective is simply: *To decide how to clear the bottleneck in production.*

The problem is that this just isn't specific enough. It sets no boundaries or conditions. It doesn't state whether there is a cost limitation, or how soon optimum production levels should be re-established. This is going to make it pretty difficult to make the right decision. You might come up with the perfect decision – except that it costs too much to implement, or takes too long. So make your objective more specific: *To decide how to clear the bottleneck in production without exceeding the annual budget, and so that normal production levels are reached within two weeks.*

 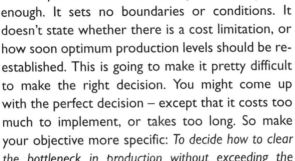

THE KEY CRITERIA

You might have any kind of preset conditions for making the right decision. You might have to find a solution that involves using two-colour printing only, or that won't interfere with coffee break times. But there are four key criteria to consider when setting your objective for any decision, and it is useful to run through them all mentally each time, to see which apply:

- ▶ cost
- ▶ time
- ▶ quality
- ▶ people – many decisions can cause upset, rifts and loss of motivation. So you may well have to decide on a course of action that won't upset a particular supplier, or that means the MD won't get wind of the problem.

If you think about it, this makes it far easier to take the decision. Too much choice always makes it tough, but once you narrow it down it's far more likely that the best option will jump out at you.

◀◀ for next time

Before you reach this stage – the point where you have to get on and take the decision – you should already be aware of the criteria you have to meet. You presumably have a file on this matter, so jot down any key criteria while you're building up the file in advance of making the decision. Make sure they really are essential preconditions, and not just desirable results.

For example, it may be essential that you clear the bottleneck in production within two weeks of your decision on how to do it. On the other hand, it may be that you'd really *like* to clear it within two weeks, but you could just about fulfil your orders if it wasn't cleared for another four weeks.

So make sure that the criteria you set down in your objective really are essential. By the time you come to set your objective, you should already know what all of them are.

Too much choice always makes it tough

2 decide to take the decision

For crying out loud! First of all we're supposed to be in a tearing hurry, and now we're expected to waste time messing about with word games. 'Decide to take the decision' – what's that supposed to mean?

Well, if you'll be patient, I'll explain. You may be in a hurry, but you could be about to waste yourself a lot of time. You wouldn't be the first person to do it. The fact is that a lot of people agonise for ages over a decision they shouldn't be taking at all. Only they haven't noticed they shouldn't be taking it.

So now you've identified exactly what your decision is – what objective it must achieve – you're in a position to double check that you really need to take it at all, before you go any further. This is actually a decision in itself, of course.

Why on earth (you may be wondering) would you decide not to take the decision? We're only here now because this decision has absolutely got to be taken, and you can't put it off any longer.

Not necessarily. There are several reasons why you might decide against going ahead. Here are the most obvious ones to consider:

▶ **It may become apparent that this is really a decision for someone else entirely. Clearing the production bottleneck might be a job for the production director, and not for you as production manager at all.**

thinkingfast

ONE-WAY TICKET TO NOWHERE

Sometimes it becomes clear at this point that the decision is impossible under the criteria you're working to. Perhaps there is no option that will enable you to clear the production bottleneck without exceeding your budget by at least 50 per cent, and one of your criteria is that you should do it within your existing budget. You won't have all the facts yet (we're doing that bit later), but you may well have enough to see that the decision isn't feasible as it stands.

In this case you should stop now. Save yourself several hours' fruitless activity. Go to your boss, or whoever has set you this impossible task, and get the criteria changed before you go any further. Otherwise you are heading straight down a decision-making dead end.

▶ Perhaps the decision is yours, but only partly. Maybe you are authorised to decide what happens to the production line, but it's up to personnel to decide how much overtime can be worked. So a joint decision will be needed to integrate these two factors.

▶ Sometimes you can resolve the issue by tackling a different or bigger problem, and thereby avoid a decision on this one altogether. Perhaps there's a proposal on the table to outsource production. If this goes ahead, you won't want to have wasted resources on clearing a bottleneck that was expensive to sort out. Maybe you're better off making a decision on a stop-gap solution, rather than on a permanent one.

▶ This decision may depend on another one that hasn't yet been made. Maybe the root of the problem is with your suppliers, who can't deliver key components ready assembled. If they did, the bottleneck would resolve itself. So in fact, you can't make a decision until you've sorted out the issue of your supplier. If the bottleneck doesn't disappear, *then* you can decide what to do about it.

▶ Maybe you should be taking the decision, but not now. Perhaps this is the busiest time of year in production and, slow as it is, the present devil you know is better than the horrendous disruption you could cause by changing the system. Better to wait, perhaps, until a quiet time of year before you get this one sorted out.

It should be clear by now that it is deeply unwise to take it for granted that you should be making this decision, or making it now. Always ask yourself whether or not to take the decision. And the answer will be a decision in itself. So once you've been through this process, you've already got one decision tucked under your belt. That should make you feel a bit better about the whole process.

for next time

You should be on the lookout for this kind of thing as soon as you plan to make a decision. If it is better not to take it, the sooner you know, the sooner you can prepare someone else to take it, or find a short-term alternative, or get on with the other decision on which this one is dependent.

And, of course, as soon as you offload or defer a decision, you cut down your own workload in the process. And I strongly suspect that's always welcome.

3 assemble the facts

$a = 2$
$b = 3$
What is $a + b$?

That was pretty simple wasn't it? (At least, it was if you reached the answer 5. If not, you're in trouble.)

   Let's try another one:

$a = 2$
$b = 3$
What is $a + c$?

Aha! Not so easy this time. In fact, downright impossible. And why? Because you simply don't have the information you need to decide on the correct answer. All you can do is make a random guess and hope it's the right one.

   It's obvious when you're doing algebra, but when it comes to making decisions, far too many managers fail to spot the obvious. They try to take decisions when they simply don't have all the information they need to find the correct solution. But just as with algebra, if you don't have all the facts, you can't expect to get the answer right.

That's why the next stage in the process is collecting together all the information you need. No matter how urgently you need to make this decision, you cannot do it without the necessary facts, or you risk making the wrong decision.

WHAT FACTS?

Collecting the facts is often the sticking point for decision makers, for one of two reasons:

- ▶ **You have far too much information, and you don't know where to start sifting it all (or you simply can't face it).**
- ▶ **You haven't got the information you need, and you can't get your head round the process of collecting it – you haven't the time, or you don't know where to go for it.**

You may well recognise one – or even both – of these. They usually explain why the decision has been put off until the last minute. So our job now is to assemble all the facts you need without tripping ourselves up on either of these stumbling blocks. And the way we go about it is the same, whether you have too much or too little information.

INFORMATION OVERLOAD

Having too much information is one of the curses of modern business. We all have piles of papers, articles, reports, books and magazines on our desk, and endless people telling us we should subscribe to this or that journal as well. But console yourself with this thought: no one else is reading all their stuff, either; they're just not admitting to it. One of today's key management skills is being able to dump loads of bumf in the bin with a clear conscience. So learn to speed read, and to select the few things you do need to read, and offload the rest. You'll go far.

The tendency is to start with the information you've got. And that's what can make the process so difficult. You need to approach the whole question of facts from the opposite angle: what information do you need?

Take a sheet of paper and divide it into two columns. Head the first column 'must know' and the second column 'prefer to know', like this:

Must know	Prefer to know

Now forget the information you actually have available, and just think about what information you need. Suppose you're trying to decide which of three suppliers of key components you're going to sign a contract with for the next 12 months. There are certain things you absolutely have to know, such as:

- ▶ their prices
- ▶ their reliability
- ▶ the quality of their components
- ▶ their billing system

... and so on.

Then there are other factors, which aren't so essential, but which may influence your decision, especially if it's fairly borderline. These could include:

- ▶ how flexible they are
- ▶ which of your competitors they supply
- ▶ how high their customer service standards are.

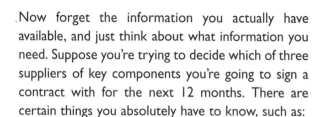

The tendency is to start with the information you've got. And that's what can make the process so difficult

BALANCING ACT

The facts that go on your 'prefer to know' list should be weighed up carefully. We know they should not be essentials, but neither should they simply be whims. For example, you might be interested to know whether you personally like the person you'd be dealing with regularly at each supplier company, but is it actually going to influence your decision in any way? Hopefully not. So don't put it down on either list.

Your list will start to shape up something like this:

Must know	Prefer to know
Price	Flexibility
Reliability	Which competitors
Quality of components	they supply
Billing system	Customer service
	standards

So now, before you've even started looking at a single report, price list, catalogue or record, you have narrowed right down to the minimum the field of information you need to bother with. If you don't need to know it, it never has to pass before your eyes at all. When you're working against the clock, this will save you a lot of time. And, as you can see, it's also a much smarter way of working.

MAKING SPACE

Leave enough space on your list to fill in the answers – or a précis of each – once you have them. This will give you a really useful single-sheet summary of key facts later on, when you come to weigh up the decision. You can staple longer documents or summary sheets from reports to the back of it, so you have all your key information in one sheaf of papers.

FINDING YOUR FACTS

So now you know what information you need, it's time to go fetch. Of course, you're limited by your time constraints, so you won't be able to do any lengthy research. There isn't time to get hold of samples of each supplier's components and test them exhaustively. Maybe you've already done this, or maybe you don't need to. But you'll be able to get most of what you need by talking to people, digging out papers from files (or from the pile on your desk), e-mailing and using the Internet. (If you need to dig out a lot of information, it's worth reading one of the other books in this series, *fast thinking: finding facts*.)

Now you know what information you need, it's time to go fetch

FACE THE FACT

If you are missing an essential piece of information that will take longer to find than you have, go back and have another look at Chapter 2. You should have decided not to take this decision now, as without essential information you cannot take the right decision (except with pot luck on your side). If you *can* manage without it, it shouldn't be in your 'must know' column, but your 'prefer to know' column.

Look at each piece of information you need to find, and think about where the best place to get it is. By best, I mean the most reliable source but also the fastest where there is a choice. In the case of the example here, I should imagine you could get most of it from the suppliers over the phone. But of course it's not always that easy.

Here's a checklist (though not an exhaustive one) of places to consider for getting the information you want:

- ▶ talking to people – suppliers, customers, experts, colleagues
- ▶ books
- ▶ competitors' annual reports
- ▶ minutes of past meetings
- ▶ internal management reports and monthly figures

- ▸ **other internal reports and survey results**
- ▸ **magazine and newspaper articles**
- ▸ **publicly available information and statistics – from trade associations, market research reports, government departments, and so on.**

You should be able to access most of these within a day, using the phone, e-mail, the Internet and your feet (at least within the building).

So the process is simple. Here's a recap:

1 List the facts you need in order to take the decision, categorising them as 'must know' or 'prefer to know'.

2 Work through your list, deciding on the best (fast) source for each piece of information.

3 Go and find each fact.

Clearly there's no point in separating your facts into two lists if you're going to treat them both the same, so you're not. The second list is not compulsory. However, in an ideal world, you should aim to collect about 80 per cent of these facts. Actually, that's not really true: in an ideal world you should collect 100 per cent of them. But in the real world, when the pressure's on, aim for

about 80 per cent. If there are some you feel would be more useful than others, you will presumably give them priority.

Having said all that, if the facts on the lists are allocated to the correct columns, it should be possible to make the right decision without any of the facts on the 'prefer to know' list. However, they will make it much easier for you to decide when the time comes. And they will, collectively, account for a significant percentage of the weight of argument, even though individually each one is not essential.

thinking fast

TIMING OUT

Obviously, you have to have all the information on your 'must know' list. That's the point of it. But the best approach to the 'prefer to know' list is to collect all the information you can quickly, but forget anything you can't find fast. One way to do this is to set yourself a time limit. If you haven't got hold of each fact on this list within a certain time, give up (unless you can see you really are almost there). The time limit is up to you, and depends on how much of a rush you're in. But try five or ten minutes as a starting point. This may mean you can abandon some facts before you even start, because you just know you won't get hold of them that fast.

FACT-FINDING PITFALLS

Some facts are easy to find, and reliable once you have them. The example of which supplier to choose might fall into this category. If you're selecting the right candidate for a job, you should have all the information you need already, once you've completed the interviews (*see fast thinking: selection interview*). But some decisions are complicated or technical (or both). For example, you might be trying to decide into which of several possible campaigns to put a large chunk of your marketing budget.

The process for assembling the facts you need is exactly the same, but there are certain pitfalls into which the unwary decision maker may fall. So here's a quick guide to alert you to the most dangerous heffalump traps in the information jungle.

Trusting statistics

Some statistical information may not be as reliable as you need it to be. For example, while you will no doubt trust figures from the Institute of Direct Marketing on the relative value of different types of campaign (advertising, direct mail or whatever), data assembled by, say, a big publishing company might be biased in favour of press advertising. A trained historian's standard question is 'Why did this document come into being?'

Aim to collect about 80 per cent of your 'prefer to know' facts

You will have to use your own judgement to decide which data to rely on – and go for the most reliable sources in the first place if you can. You will also have to make up your own mind how much it matters. If you think a certain figure may be slightly biased but you only need a ballpark estimate, perhaps you will decide to use the figures anyway. The important thing is to recognise when the data you're using is not wholly reliable.

Making assumptions.

It's frighteningly easy to do this without even knowing it. Many managers fall into the trap of thinking they know more than they do. It's easy to see it with the more overconfident, arrogant type, but even charming, humble people like us do it sometimes. The problem is, we have a fair amount of experience of our subject, so we assume our 'knowledge' is reliable. For example, as a marketing person, it's easy to think 'direct mail is better targeted than advertising, so it's got to be a more cost-effective option.'

You may be right but, then again, you may not. So do the research and verify your assumptions, otherwise you could go very wrong. If you collect (or assume) misinformation, you're almost bound to make a wrong decision. Lord Kelvin, an eminent scientist who was president of the Royal Society at the end of the nineteenth century, has gone down in history for saying 'Heavier-than-air flying machines are impossible.' Presumably he was making inaccurate assumptions to arrive at this conclusion.

Treating estimates as facts

It's often necessary to make your own calculations of the probability of a certain outcome, in order to feed this information into your decision-making process. You might want to calculate, for example, the income from a direct mail campaign. You're going to have to estimate certain figures to work on, such as the likely response rate, the size of the mailing and so on. You'll have checked your estimates, of course, and you'll judge the best figures to use. But it's very easy to start taking these figures as gospel.

Suppose you've assumed a 7 per cent response to your mailing. You know how many customers you're going to mail, and you know your average order value. Anyway, you can do several calculations for different sizes of mailings. And for different order values. The danger is that you will forget that your response rate of 7 per cent is only a best guess. If you treat it as a fact rather than an estimate, you may rely too heavily on your calculations. So remember that the response rate might turn out to be 8 per cent, or only 5 per cent.

WORD OF WARNING

Research indicates that our minds are unconsciously biased towards whatever estimate we settle on, even though we know it is only an estimate. So if you decide to estimate a response rate of 7 per cent to your mailshot you are likely to find, if you have the sense to remember that it's only an estimate, that you calculate for anywhere between 5 and 9 per cent. Very wise. But the true figure might actually have been 2 per cent, or 14 per cent. Your initial estimate anchors you to it, and can close your mind to wider options. So look out.

Looking for information that doesn't exist

Believe it or not, even in this electronic age, there are some pieces of information that have never been recorded. Or if they have, you ain't never gonna find them. You can waste hours or even days looking for stuff that isn't there. Some managers even put off decisions to the point of causing major disruption, because they are holding out for information that doesn't exist. And sometimes, it is even information on your 'must know' list that you can't track down.

The sooner you can recognise that the information simply isn't going to materialise, the sooner you can find an alternative and get on and make your decision. Think about those heavier-than-air flying machines again. The early inventors could feed in all the scientific data available, but I can tell you what would be top of my 'must know' list: is this thing going to fly or not? And there is no way that information is available until *after* you've made the decision on whether or not to jump from the top of the tallest building with the thing strapped to your back.

So face it. If the information isn't there, stop looking. Collect all the information you can to make a best possible estimate, and settle for that.

At the end of this stage, you should have collected all the facts you need to make the decision. And I hope you'll be feeling a whole lot happier. But although you may have all the hard facts, there's still one more ingredient you need: other people's input. That's what the next chapter is all about.

for next time

Some facts take longer to collect than others, so give yourself plenty of time for the information that it will take a while to pull together. Maybe you need to get it from other people who are hard to pin down, or maybe you need to run tests or trials and feed the results in to your decision.

The more time you allow, the easier it is to delegate fact-finding, too. It's pretty difficult to free up someone to dig out data for you at a moment's notice, but tell them you don't need it for a fortnight and suddenly they are much more cooperative.

4 consult

Winston Churchill would never have taken a key decision without consulting his Cabinet and his military advisers. Julius Caesar listened to advice (although famously he didn't take it from the soothsayer). Napoleon consulted his generals. But some managers think they can make key decisions all by themselves.

Well you can't. You almost always need to consult other people before you make any important decision, and especially one that will affect them. You need to do this for two reasons:

1 **To collect their input and opinions**. There's every chance that someone else will know something you don't, or will have thought of an option that you hadn't. Or perhaps you need to know that if you make a particular decision the whole of accounts is going to be up in arms, or production will slow down by 5 per cent.

2 **To make them feel included and involved**. If people who are affected by your decision feel that they haven't had an opportunity to put their case,

they are likely to be resentful of any decision that doesn't exactly suit them. Lack of consultation can lead to general demotivation and frustration and, of course, people will be far less committed to a decision they feel they had no part in.

WHO TO CONSULT?

So who are you going to talk to about this decision? Well, obviously the people who you think are most likely to have something useful to say about it. This might mean colleagues, outside experts, your own team, your senior managers, your customers or your suppliers. Phoning an IT expert is a form of consultation, just as much as calling a team meeting to discuss the issue.

Think about who might have information you don't know about, or don't know you need. For example,

thinking smart

GET THE BOSS ON BOARD

Whether or not your boss has to approve your decision, it is always better to involve them in the process. Not only are they likely to have a useful input, but they are much more likely to back your decision if they feel they contributed towards it.

QUALITY NOT QUANTITY

The more people you consult, the longer it will take. So when time is as precious as it is now, think carefully about whose input you most need. Look for a spread of expertise between your advisers, rather than talking to several people who are likely to cover much the same ground.

maybe your predecessor as marketing manager might be happy to talk to you about previous campaigns and what did and didn't work – whether they are still in the organisation or not. But you are not simply fact-finding here – the information is doubtless on record anyway. You are looking for interpretations of those facts from your predecessor: why did this campaign work and that one fail?

GO TO THE TOP

However pushed for time you are, don't exclude anyone who is likely to be upset by a controversial decision. However, you don't have to consult every last person. If another department is going to be affected by your decision, consult the department head. It is their responsibility to collect input from their team, if they want to, and pass it on to you.

If your decision is relatively uncontroversial, consulting is easier. When you speak to senior colleagues or outsiders, a phone call will often do the trick. But if anyone is likely to be upset by the outcome of your decision, or if they will be deeply affected by it, always consult them formally. This means three things:

1 Agree a time and place to discuss the issue face-to-face.

2 Give them as much warning as you can.

3 Talk to them alone.

Right now, the time and place may be your office in half an hour. But the more time people have to

thinking smart

PHONE VERSUS E-MAIL

You can ask people's advice or opinions by e-mail – and if you're in a hurry it may be the only way. Speaking face to face or by phone is better if you can manage it – it gives you a chance to question and listen to nuances of tone. On the other hand, you can blanket e-mail a lot of people quickly if you want a quick 'yes/no' or 'pick option A or B' type response from a lot of people. So pick the best medium for the job.

There's every chance that someone else will know something you don't prepare, the more satisfied they will feel that they've had a chance to put their case to you properly. An element of formality reassures them that you are taking their views seriously. If you simply stop someone in the corridor and say: 'By the way, which floor do you reckon your department should get when we move to the new offices?' they may not even realise they've been consulted.

LISTENING IS NOT THE SAME AS FOLLOWING

Just because you listen to someone's advice, it doesn't mean to say you have to take it. This is your decision, it's not being taken by vote. There's no point asking anyone for a view if you're not going to take account of it, but neither should you follow it for the sake of it. After all, you are the one in possession of all the necessary facts, and you know what the other people you've consulted have said, too.

thinking smart

LESS IS MORE

The more opinions you ask, the more likely they are to conflict with each other. So don't let it get to the point where you simply become confused (as if you had the time to talk to that many people, anyway). You avoided information overload successfully when you assembled your facts; stick to the same approach here.

However, make a note of what the people you've consulted have said; you'll be needing it later (as you'll see when you get to Chapter 7). You will also want to feed these views into your final decision making, by which time you may have forgotten who said what, or even what it was they said. It may make a big difference to know from whom a certain opinion came, or exactly what the opinion was. What's more, they may have forgotten what they said, and your notes will serve to remind you both if they deny they said it. So jot it down, and keep it with your sheet of ready facts.

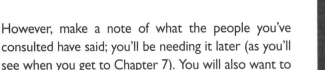

for next time

If you allow more time for consultation, it opens up new possibilities. You might get in a firm of consultants to advise you on the departmental reorganisation before you make the final decision. If you're really pushed for time, phoning someone in the USA or Australia might be out simply because you haven't got time to get hold of them. A little more time could have been a big help.

More time is also a huge advantage for a controversial decision. If you consult people this afternoon and then announce your decision tomorrow morning, they are likely to feel you had already made up your mind and the consultation was only a token one. And there's the danger that they will feel they haven't had the opportunity to prepare. So consult well in advance, especially where the decision is likely to provoke an emotional response.

5 identify the options

Many people reach this stage and then make their decision intuitively. Once they have all the information and input, they simply decide. This is certainly fast, but we set out to reach the *right* decision, if you remember, not just a fast one. So we're going to do this properly.

Having said that, an intuitive decision is fine at this point for small decisions, such as where to hold next week's appraisal interviews or how to organise your filing cabinet (the earlier stages won't have taken long, either). You haven't got time to go through a methodical decision-making process 20 times a day. But I don't imagine you bought this book to help you with that sort of decision.

If your decision is important enough to be reading this book, it's important enough to get right. And research has shown time and again that a methodical approach gives you a better chance of making the right decision than intuition does – although it often seems otherwise because we tend to be happy to live with wrong decisions taken on gut feeling.

You've done all the preparation, and you can now begin to make your decision. And the very first thing you have to do is to identify your options. These are what you'll be deciding between, so you'd better know what they are.

Some options will be obvious, of course. You knew all along that one of the options for cutting down on company cars was to provide them only for employees who travel as part of their job. And another option was to leave things as they are. But a classic error many decision makers commit is to limit their options. Too often, they give themselves an either/or choice. So the first thing to do is to come up with more options.

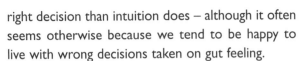

thinking smart

THE VALUE OF INTUITION
If you are one of those people who has a strong sense of intuition, and confidence in your own gut feelings, you certainly shouldn't disregard these. However, don't rely on them to the exclusion of all else. If the decision matters, it's worth putting all your resources into getting it right, not leaving it to intuition alone.

GIVE ME MORE

Alfred Sloan, the former president of General Motors (and universally acknowledged as one of the greatest businessmen of all time), had a habit of adjourning meetings in which he was presented with an either/or choice. He would insist that his executives went away until they could come up with more options.

In the case of the company cars, there could be other routes you might take; maybe someone else has suggested another option to you during your consultation period. For example, how about:

▶ letting anyone who already has a company car keep it, but not allowing anyone else to have one (unless they need it to work)

▶ giving employees a travel allowance instead of a car

▶ giving company cars only to people who have been with the organisation for more than five years.

All of these ideas cut down the total expenditure on company cars, and you now have five options instead of two. That has to equip you better for making the best decision.

11 **thinking smart**

THE FORGOTTEN OPTION

Remember that doing nothing is often one of your options.

KEEP IT FEASIBLE

You want to give yourself as many options as you can, within reason. That is to say that 500 options is more than you can deal with (especially in the time you've got left), but half a dozen – at this stage – is certainly better than only two.

However, there's no point generating just any options, however unrealistic. You need to come up with feasible options. Setting your objective right at the beginning will help with this – you're looking for options that fit the objective, including any constraints such as cost or time. But some options that fit the objective clearly aren't feasible. For example, there's not a lot of point suggesting that employees share company cars one to every six employees, so each one has the car for a month and then passes it on.

The very first thing you have to do is to identify your options. Give yourself as many options as you can, within reason

❚❚ DON'T GET BOGGED DOWN

You don't have to conduct a detailed feasibility study on every option at this stage – we'll do that later if it needs doing at all. Just think briefly through each option to make sure that it isn't obviously unfeasible.

GENERATING OPTIONS

So how exactly are you supposed to come up with all these options? You have very little time to play with here, and suddenly you're supposed to generate ideas at the drop of a hat. That's right. Your thinking hat. It's time to put it on and come up with some creative ideas.

If there was only one, blindingly obvious option open to you, you'd have made the decision weeks ago, wouldn't you? You're in this position because the best course of action isn't clear to you. Perhaps none of the options seems very appealing. In these situations a highly creative, unexpected solution can often turn out to be the best. But you have to think of it first.

If you think you're not creative, you may feel yourself starting to panic at this point. You're not really an ideas person. Only hours to go and you've got to come up with new, fresh and creative solutions. You can't do it, can you?

> ### BELIEVE IT
> One of the keys to arriving at creative answers is the belief
> that there is a solution. The psychological effect of doubting
> that the answer exists is strong enough to prevent you
> finding it. Henry Ford said: 'Whether you believe you can, or
> whether you believe you can't, you're absolutely right.' So be
> confident: the answer is out there and you're going to find it.

Of course you can. We're all capable of being highly
creative, if we know how to be. Creativity is a skill
you can learn. Sure, some people find it comes
more naturally than others do, but we can all learn
it – and fast (which may be more to the point right
now). All you need is a few creative techniques for
generating ideas quickly.

Problem reversal

This is a quick and easy creativity technique. All
you have to do is to phrase your problem – 'we're
spending too much on company cars' – and then
reverse it. So you get 'we're not spending enough
on company cars'. Now try to think of solutions to
this reversed problem. How about these:

⊳ **We should buy bigger and better cars for everyone.**

If there was only one option open to you, you'd have made the decision weeks ago

▶ We should give company cars to everyone, right down to the part-time cafeteria trainee.

▶ We should give some employees two cars.

You might be wondering where this has got you. Well, it's opened up new channels of thinking, that's what. You can now look at these apparently barmy ideas and use them to generate new and feasible ideas to the real problem:

▶ The idea of bigger and better cars might give you the idea of grading the type of cars you give people. Long service enables you to progress from a much cheaper car than the present standard to a much better one. If you grade the progress correctly the overall bill will be cheaper, but the cars are still there, and so is the motivation to stay with the company.

▶ Company cars for absolutely everyone could lead you to think of other forms of transport. Perhaps you could give junior people bicycles (depending on your location). Or you could have a collective form of transport. If you're five miles, from the nearest station, you could run a company shuttle bus to and from it each morning and evening.

▶ Two cars per employee sounds daft, but what about two employees per car? What about allocating cars to certain people on the condition that they use it to give other employees who live nearby a free lift to and from work?

> ## QUANTITY EQUALS QUALITY
>
> One of the best things about creativity is that whoever you are – Einstein or just an ordinary mortal like the rest of us – the number of good ideas you have will be a fairly consistent proportion of the total. Einstein had more good ideas than most of us, but then he had more bad ideas too. The point was that he just had lots of them. So the route to having good ideas is simply to generate plenty. If one idea in ten is good, you're better off having 200 ideas than just 20.

You see, this is a quick and simple technique for coming up with some original options. Everyone is different – you would probably have come up with different solutions from the same problem reversal. That's fine. So long as you generate original and realistic ideas, you have a better chance of making the right decision.

Random stimulation

Like most creativity techniques, this one's fun too. And fast. The idea is really to knock your mind sideways into a different way of thinking – so you come up with different ideas from last time.

Start by selecting a word at random. Try opening a dictionary with your eyes shut, pointing at a

The idea is really to knock your mind sideways into a different way of thinking

word, and then opening your eyes. This is the word you have to work with. If you haven't got a dictionary to hand, pick the name of the first object you see, or take a random word from another book. Suppose you pick the word 'sugar'. Now think about sugar for a while:

- ▶ It's sweet.
- ▶ It comes from a plant.
- ▶ It comes in lumps or grains.
- ▶ You can eat it.
- ▶ There are lots of varieties.
- ▶ It makes you fat.

It's up to you what attributes of sugar you come up with. You don't have to be comprehensive. After thinking about it for a while, go back to your company car problem and think about the two things in tandem – sugar and company cars. See how thinking about sugar can help to stimulate ideas:

- ▶ Lots of varieties might lead you to a much wider range of company vehicles, planned to reduce the overall bill. Perhaps you could offer everyone a bicycle, certain people a travel allowance, further up the scale people could qualify for a small second-hand car, and on up to a Rolls for the MD.

STAY COOL

Although these techniques are effective whatever your mood, you will find that the more you can relax the better you free up your unconscious mind to generate creative ideas for you. I know this isn't a great moment to say this with a crucial decision impending but ... try to relax.

▶ Eating sugar might take your mind on to corporate entertaining, and expense accounts. Perhaps you could offset company cars against the expense account – the more expensive the car, the lower the expenses allowance.

▶ Sugar makes you fat, and so does driving – compared with walking, jogging or cycling. Perhaps you could get rid of the company cars as part of a corporate fitness campaign. Spend some of the savings on putting in a really good gym in the basement, and offer a free bicycle to anyone who wants it. That way, you may be taking away with one hand, but you're giving with the other.

Sensory images

One more for now, and then it's time to get on with making your decision. All you do here is think about your five senses in relation to the problem, and see if any of them helps to generate an idea. What does the idea of 'sound' in relation to company cars make you think of, for example? It can help to sit back, close your eyes and relax for this technique (if you can). Here are a couple of ideas:

- sound. If you take away people's company cars, give them a really good sound system to put into the car they have to buy for themselves as a compensation.

- smell. This might make you think of the smell of leather seats. How about another form of compensation? Why not upgrade the offices of employees who lose their company cars: large-screen monitors, swivel leather armchair, that sort of thing?

Hypnogogic imagery

This technique works well for many people, but you have to be tired enough to go to sleep (you don't actually have to have a nap – I doubt you have time). Or you may be able to wait until bedtime to do it.

Hypnogogic images are those dream images you see as you are starting to drift into sleep, but before you completely lose consciousness. The idea is to close your eyes, relax and clear your mind of any other thoughts. Then focus on the decision you have to make, and on the question you want answered: how can I reduce spending on company cars?

As you think about the problem, allow your mind to wander towards sleep and to generate its own images. Just before you fall asleep, rouse yourself and record the images before you forget them. Very often, your unconscious mind will show you the solution to your problem.

You can vary this technique – if time allows – by actually falling asleep and recording your dreams when you awake. This method is commonly known as 'sleeping on it', and it really can work. One of the best examples is the guy who invented the sewing machine (a chap called Elias Howe). He was having problems with the design of the needle, which he couldn't get to work. One night, he dreamt he was attacked by a band of savages carrying spears. The spears all had holes in the tips. Howe realised when he woke that this was the answer to his problem;

thinking smart

DIY ALARM

If you're thinking of trying hypnogogic imagery as a technique, you may have noticed the flaw in the system. How can you be sure you'll wake yourself up in time, rather than simply fall asleep and stay that way? Salvador Dali had an ingenious solution to this (you won't be surprised, considering his paintings, to know that he was fond of this technique). He used to doze in a chair holding a spoon in his hand. On the floor below it was a metal plate. As soon as he fell asleep he naturally relaxed his grip, the spoon would fall and hit the plate, and the noise would wake him up.

As you think about the problem allow your mind to wander towards sleep. Very often, your unconscious mind will show you the solution to your problem the hole should go in the tip of the needle, not in the other end as it does on an ordinary needle.

Drawing techniques

The creative function is located in the right side of the brain, along with visual perception, while verbal skills are handled in the left brain. So if you use visual rather than verbal techniques, they can connect with your creative powers more readily since they are closer together. This is why many people find that doodling and drawing are more creative than verbal techniques.

One of the simplest methods is simply to draw the challenge as you see it. To decide how to handle the company cars problem, maybe you draw cars all over the page, or someone tearing up banknotes, or irate staff waiting on station platforms. You might doodle bicycles everywhere, or lots of people balancing on one car. Everyone's drawings and doodles will be different, but as you focus on the problem and draw whatever comes into your head, you often find you've stimulated an idea that gives you a new option.

Doodles are more abstract than drawings, and some people find this freeform approach more stimulating. The idea is to concentrate on the decision you need to make and simply doodle at random. When you've filled the page, look at what you've drawn and somewhere in it you should see something which gives you a new perspective on the decision in front of you.

Some people like to experiment by creating different doodles. You can do this by, for example:

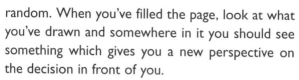

- ▶ **Using coloured pens, paints or even finger painting – whatever you fancy**
- ▶ **Doodling with your eyes closed**
- ▶ **Using the other hand from usual to draw with**

RING THE CHANGES

Well, you should have more options on the table now than you had a few minutes ago. I'm not suggesting you use all these techniques – at least, not right now. Use whichever appeals to you. And then use a different one next time. If you always use the same technique your mind will get stuck in a rut, and the creativity level will start to drop off. So vary your methods. There are plenty more you can learn about if you want to – buy a book on the subject.

By now you should have a list of at least four or five perfectly valid options to decide between. So now you have all your ingredients ready, let's get cooking.

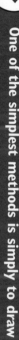

Given a little more time, one of the very best ways to produce a list of options is to call together a group of colleagues for half an hour – perhaps your own team – and brainstorm a list. Between about half a dozen and a dozen people is the optimum number. We've all heard of brainstorming, and we know the gist. Everyone comes up with as many ideas as possible and you write them down on a board or flip chart.

But to get the best out of brainstorming, you need to follow the rules. If you didn't realise there were rules, you're not alone. But they are designed to maximise the number of ideas the session generates. There are just four of them:

1 No one is allowed to judge or criticise any idea. This is the most important rule of all. If people start to criticise, it inhibits others from making suggestions for fear of ridicule. And since the wackiest ideas can often be the best, it will probably cost you some of your most promising ideas.

2 All ideas are welcome, no matter how off the wall. The strangest ideas are the ones that open up everyone's creativity. Even if they aren't feasible in themselves, they often lead to really useful, feasible ideas.

3 The more ideas the better. Quantity generates quality.

4 No idea is sacred – aim to combine ideas, refine them or build on ideas already put forward, as well as generating new ones.

It's your job, as group leader, to make sure all these rules are adhered to. So next time you're in this position, give yourself time to call a brainstorming session. You should find it fun, exhilarating and highly productive.

If you always use the same technique your mind will get stuck in a rut, and the creativity level will start to drop off

6 decision time

You're on the home straight now. You've collected all the facts you need, and you've generated a list of options. Now you simply have to decide which is the best one. Sometimes, by the time you get to this stage, the right decision will have become clear. But even when it hasn't, the odds are that you can see it comes down to one of only two or three options, and you can discard the rest.

The best approach to reaching the right decision is to adopt a process of elimination. Suppose you started with six or seven options. Once you've done all your preparation – assembling facts and consulting other people – it should be easy to narrow this down to a list of three or maybe four. Then you simply go through them all – using the techniques in this chapter – and keep knocking out options as you establish that they are less good than any of the others. It won't be long before

WITHOUT PREJUDICE

When you're considering options, you may have to be strict with yourself about ignoring any personal prejudice. You might prefer a particular decision because that option was your idea. Or you might dislike certain options because you or your department will not do so well out of them. For example, if you're considering what to do about company cars, you might be tempted to go for an option that allows *you* to keep your company car. But force yourself to disregard such personal bias, and weigh up your options objectively.

you're down to just one option – or perhaps two (we'll look at what to do when you have two equal options later on).

EVALUATING THE OPTIONS

You need to look at each option in turn in order to establish its merits. You'll want to use the notes you assembled with all the facts – or a précis of each – on a single sheet, with fuller details attached. And you should keep your objective written down in front of you all the time as a reminder of what your winning option must measure up to.

The most important thing you need to establish is the level of risk and reward involved in each option.

Consider this for each option – we'll see how in a moment. Beyond that – if that alone doesn't make your decision clear – there are various methods you can choose from to help you make your mind up. But we'll start with the risk/reward evaluation.

This is the most important evaluation for every viable option. You cannot decide which is the best course of action until you know what might result from it. So you need to examine the potential negative results *and* the potential positive ones. The simplest way to do this is to envisage the worst possible and best possible scenarios.

thinking smart

EXPERIENCE VERSUS SCIENCE

Lots of text books will give you mathematical formulae for calculating risk, and of course risk assessment is a career in itself. But for the vast majority of non-technical management decisions, you won't need all that maths. Your own experience and unbiased judgement are far more relevant for deciding which candidate to appoint to the job, or how to resolve the overcrowding problem in the accounts offices. Even deciding whether to sink your whole marketing budget into one major campaign, or whether to spread it between several smaller ones, will rely far more on your knowledge of marketing than of maths.

For each option, write down the worst thing that could possibly happen as a result: production would grind to a halt, you'd lose a major contract, the wrong person in the job would be less effective and leave sooner, you'd have wasted half your budget, the building would collapse.

Next to this, write down the best possible scenario: productivity would double, your best customer would become more committed to you, the right person in the job would revolutionise its effectiveness, you'd have doubled the income generated by your department, morale and productivity would rocket as a result of brighter, bigger, more sociable offices.

There are two more points to make about the risk/reward evaluation before you can draw any conclusions from it:

- ▷ **The risk and the reward are balanced at either end of a see-saw.**
- ▷ **The likelihood of these scenarios taking place is also a factor.**

Let's look at each of these in turn.

The see-saw

You are not simply considering the scenarios here in isolation – you have to look at how they balance each other. A very high risk might be worthwhile if the other end of the see-saw gives a very high reward. If the worst possible scenario involves a risk of imprisonment for several of your senior directors, you can rule out that option (I'm afraid) regardless of the potential rewards.

In fact, a very high potential risk often rules an option out, but it shouldn't always. Many of the most successful decisions ever made have involved an element of high risk – this is often the pay-off for a high reward.

thinking smart

HIGH RISK, HIGH REWARD

Walt Disney was balancing a high risk against a high reward when he decided to make the cartoon *Snow White*. No one had ever made a feature-length cartoon before, and many people thought it would flop; no one could sit through 90 minutes of cartoon, surely? What's more, it cost so much to make that if it *had* flopped, the Disney studio would have folded. There's your high risk. In fact, of course, the reward when it succeeded was massive, and clearly had been worth the risk.

Likelihood

You obviously need to take into account the likelihood of the worst and best possible scenarios actually happening. If the worst possible scenario is pretty bad, but the odds on it happening are minimal, it might well still be a viable option. You'll be balancing it against the potential reward, too, and if this is both high and likely, the option still looks promising. Set against a lower reward, which is also fairly unlikely, the option seems less appealing.

You might like to estimate the likelihood of each scenario and pencil it in on your notes. Bear in mind that it's only a very rough guide, but give it marks out of ten, or a percentage, if this helps you to weigh the balance. And remember that the two added together don't have to come to 100 per cent. The actual outcome might be somewhere in between these two. It may well be that you estimate the worst possible outcome as a 10 per cent likelihood, and the best as around 20 per cent. In other words, the most likely outcome is neither of these.

So you can see that the balance of risk and reward, and their relative likelihoods, have to be factored in before you can evaluate the option properly. At the end of your risk/reward evaluation, you can eliminate some of your options:

▶ **where the potential risk is high but the reward is low**

- ▶ where the potential risk is insupportable, such as a risk of personal injury or, worse, to other people

- ▶ where the likelihood of the worst possible scenario is significantly greater than the likelihood of the best possible outcome.

OTHER TYPES OF EVALUATION

You may well find at the end of the risk/reward evaluation that your course is clear. At the very least, you should have narrowed down your options. After all, as soon as you can see that an option isn't the best, just strike it off the list. You don't have to prove it's unworkable or would be catastrophic. But you want a list that contains only those options that you still think might turn out to be the best. By now, there should be only two or perhaps three possibilities left.

So how are you going to eliminate all but one of these? Different methods of evaluating work well for different people, so choose one that you feel comfortable with. Some of us like to rely heavily on intuition (although you're trying to resist that for the moment), some like to weigh everything precisely, some worry deeply about the risks, while others are inclined to overconfidence when we fix our sights on the potential rewards.

You want to get on with this decision now because time's running out, so we're not going to bother with long, complex methods of assessment that involve drawing graphs and matrices filled with figures, or flow charts that occupy most of one wall. The approaches here are simple and straightforward, and will work for all but the most complex technical or financial decisions.

Write down notes as you work through whichever method (or methods) you choose on your 'master sheet' on which you've already noted your risk/reward evaluation for each option.

thinking fast

DON'T WASTE TIME

You probably don't need to be told this when time is precious, but you need to match the time you put into this process to both the importance and the complexity of the decision. If the decision is not of huge importance, don't waste two days evaluating it when an hour or two would get you to much the same answer. Equally, a simple decision (in other words, non-technical and without complex ramifications) simply doesn't justify several hours of your time after you've identified the options.

A complex and important decision, on the other hand, can demand hours or even days of evaluation – but if you've left it this late I don't imagine that's what you're dealing with right now (I certainly hope not). So assess how much time the decision needs and warrants before you bury yourself in lengthy evaluations.

Thinking through the consequences

The risk/reward evaluation looked only at the opposite ends of the scale of possible outcomes. As such, it makes an excellent instant eliminator round. However, it's now time to look at the consequences in more detail – not only the best and worst but those in between as well.

The risk/reward evaluation looked at the *possible* results of your decision. This approach, however, not only takes a less extreme approach but it also looks at the *known* results rather than the possibles. All you need to do is to note down everything that you know will result if you choose each given option.

Note down the consequences in two columns: positive and negative. And think through all the areas where there will be consequences. For example, there may be consequences for:

- ▶ **the organisation**
- ▶ **the department**
- ▶ **you**
- ▶ **the budget**
- ▶ **production schedules**

... and so on. And don't forget to include the emotional consequences. If you know that despatch will be very upset by a particular decision, put this down on your list.

So when you've finished working through the option of giving your top customer an unprecedentedly big discount, your list might look like this:

Positive	Negative
It will increase the customer's loyalty	It will cut margins
It will guarantee bulk sales	It will set a precedent with this customer
It will improve the stage payment arrangements	
Production will be easier to schedule	

Remember, you're writing down what you know, not what you think *might happen*. Concentrate on the direct and certain consequences of your decision. So, for example, you haven't included the point that it will set a precedent with other customers if they get wind of it, because you don't *know* that they will.

You will find that going through this thought process is as valuable as having the result of it on paper in front of you. And with any luck, by the end of it, you'll have knocked another option or two on the head.

DON'T HOLD BACK

Almost every decision involves an element of uncertainty. If you wait until you can guarantee the outcome, you'll never make the decision – which may be as damaging as the outcome you fear that is holding you back. So get as close to certainty as you reasonably can (even if it's not as close as you'd like), and then just go for it.

List the pros and cons

This technique is similar to the last, but not the same. You're listing arguments in favour and against, rather than listing consequences. However, the consequences obviously feed the arguments.

You will end up with a more comprehensive list this way. But balance that against the fact that it will contain fewer certainties and more predictions. Let's try the same option again: to give your major customer the big discount they're demanding.

Pro	Con
The customer's layout should increase	It will cut margins
The bulk sales will be guaranteed	It will set a precedent with this customer
The stage payments will be better than otherwise	It may set a precedent with other customers if they find out about it
Production will be easier to schedule	Our suppliers will give us good bulk discounts to offset the cost of our discount, but they may not maintain them
They are likely to increase their order in future if the price to them has reduced	If we hit serious production or delivery problems, our margins could be cut severely, or even wiped out

As you can see, you now have far more positive and negative points than you had with the previous 'consequences' technique. On the other hand, those were certain, and many of these are only guesses. You may prefer one or other of these techniques, or you might like to try both – assuming you have time. Once you've tried them both, you'll generally find in future that you only

Make sure you always apply the same technique to all the options

need to use one, and you can choose whichever seems most appropriate. Just make sure you always apply the same technique to all the options. Don't use 'consequences' for option A and 'pros and cons' for option B.

Can I sleep at night?

This technique really is called Can I Sleep At Night (CISAN for short). What you do is ask yourself, for each option: 'What will I most regret if I take this option?' And then: 'What will I most regret if I don't take it?' (The idea is to ask if you'd be able to sleep at night if you did or didn't choose each option.)

Suppose you're trying to decide which of your top two candidates for the post of PR assistant you will appoint. For candidate A, ask yourself these two questions:

thinking smart

NEGATIVES ARE EASIER TO PROVE

When you're examining whether a course of action will or won't work, remember that it is always easier to prove a negative than a positive. In other words, you may well be able to prove an option is not going to succeed, but you are far less likely to find conclusive proof that it will. So be prepared to settle for the fact that absence of negative proof may be as good as it gets.

- ▶ *What will I most regret if I appoint this candidate?* You might answer that you'll regret committing yourself to putting in a lot of time to training up someone with huge potential but minimal experience.

- ▶ *What will I most regret if I don't appoint this candidate?* Perhaps you'll regret not appointing someone who has a natural confidence and rapport with people – an important quality in a PR person.

Now repeat the questions for candidate B. This approach often throws up a new angle on the decision that you hadn't previously considered. Not only that but, as you'll have realised, it's a really quick technique.

Involve others

You should be getting pretty close by now to seeing which option is the best one to take. However, if you're still troubled by the choice, there's no rule that says you can't ask advice. You consulted with other people to draw up your list of options – so now do it again if it helps.

You should find – especially given the time constraint at the moment – that you only need to talk to one or possibly two people. Or you might call in a small group of two or three immediate team colleagues for a quick meeting. Either way, simply pick

There's no rule that says you can't ask advice

up the phone and ask if you can have a few minutes of their time (over the phone or face to face). Then simply outline the options and ask them if they can see whether one is better than the other, and why.

Discuss it with them if it helps, but if they have no clear view there's not a lot of point wasting everyone's time going round in circles. You can do that much more quickly by yourself. So don't go for a long meeting – just ten or fifteen minutes at most to see if they can raise any important points you'd overlooked.

MAKING YOUR CHOICE

You've done everything you can to arrive at the best decision (and in a short time), and the chances are that you can now see which way to go. If at this stage you still really can't choose between the last

thinking smart

SLEEP ON IT

The old trick of sleeping on a decision really does work. It gives your unconscious mind the opportunity to rearrange all the pieces into a pattern that makes sense. You may wake up with a blinding realisation of which choice to go for. Even if you don't, the picture may be much clearer by morning. So if you can leave the decision until tomorrow morning, do.

two options, just toss a coin. No, seriously. If it's that close a call, it doesn't matter which you decide on. Never forget the importance of making the decision as a factor in itself. Putting it off may be worse than any of the other options.

There's another thing that can occasionally happen at this point: you don't like any of the options. None of them seems very promising, so what do you do? In this case, you will have to settle for the 'least worst' option. Not much fun, but there it is. A decision has to be made, and the best decision – even if uninspiring – is still the best.

Bear in mind, however, that the least worst option might be to do nothing at all, and simply leave things as they are. However, making a firm decision that this is what you will do is still far better than leaving things alone simply because you haven't made the decision yet. This way everyone knows where they stand, and can get on with making decisions that were waiting on yours. So you still need to commit to a firm decision to do nothing.

By now you know which option you want to take, and there's just one more thing you have to do: commit to it totally. The time for dithering is over, and you must now throw your weight 100 per cent behind your decision. Yes, even if you only arrived at it by tossing a coin, or if it's a least worst option that you didn't want to have to choose. If you – its originator – aren't behind it, you can be sure as hell no one else will be.

So be totally committed yourself, and you can then transmit that commitment to everyone else when you communicate the decision to them, which is the next and final stage.

for next time

If your decision is complicated, or has many ramifications, you will need to leave yourself longer to reach it. You may even think through the consequences and then want to make secondary decisions along the 'what if ...' route to check that it is still feasible. For example, you might decide that option A for clearing your production bottleneck looks best, but there's a danger the machine you'd have to install might become obsolete within a couple of years. So what if you need spares for it after that?

At this stage – given enough time – you can decide what you will do if this happens. You shouldn't waste a lot of time on 'what if' decisions – they may never happen – but you may need to get far enough to establish that you will be able to find a workable solution if you need to.

Even with less complex decisions, it's always worth at least allowing yourself enough time to sleep on a decision, or to mull it over if you need to. Time away from the decision after you've evaluated the option can be a huge help. When you come back to it, everything slots into place. So schedule in a day or two's gap between evaluating the options and making the final decision.

It's always worth allowing yourself enough time to sleep on a decision

7

communicate
your decision

You've made your decision, and you can breathe a sigh of relief. Well done! But the job's not over yet. You've still got to tell everyone else. And not only tell them, but get their support too. So you need to find the right way to tell them, and then you have to sell them the decision and convince them it really is the best one, even if they aren't happy with some of its effects.

Needless to say, if people were consulted in the first place, they will be far more likely to go along with your decision now even if it isn't the one they want. They will feel they had their say, and that you took their views into account.

You will realise, when you read this chapter, that you will have to spend a few minutes preparing what you're going to say to everyone before you walk into the briefing session.

WHO TO TELL

Many managers make a big mistake at this stage: they don't tell enough people about their decision. If you want people on your side, the very first thing to do is show them they are important enough to hear the decision from you personally. If you let them hear it from someone else, it signals that you didn't consider them important. And that's not a good start if you want their commitment.

So tell everybody, whether they are senior or junior to you, who is going to be affected by this decision. Tell everyone that you consulted. And if you're in any doubt at all about whether you need to tell certain people, err on the side of caution and tell them anyway.

HOW TO TELL THEM

Ever heard of the grapevine? Of course you have. And the best way to feed the grapevine is to talk to people individually or in small groups. Then they have plenty opportunities to say: 'Well, I heard …', and 'Ooh, no, that's not what I was told …', and 'Apparently, according to Pat …' and so on. Everyone will have a different version of the decision, rumours will fly, and the grapevine will be at its most fruitful.

If people were consulted in the first place, they will be far more likely to go along with your decision now

Or you could do it properly. Get everyone together and brief them collectively. That means that everyone hears the same version of events, at the same time, from the same person. It gives the poor grapevine precious little chance to flourish. (And it's far quicker than telling people individually – you only have to go through it all once.)

WHAT TO TELL THEM

So you've decided who to tell, and you've collected them all together. Now what are you going to say to them? Well, obviously you're going to tell them what you've decided. But there's more to it than that. You can't just call everyone together and say: 'Right, all of you, I've decided that you've all got to wear uniforms from now on. Off you go now, and pick up your new outfits from the box by the door on your way out.'

thinking smart

FLATTERY WILL GET YOU FAR

Since telling everyone at once involves a meeting of some sort, there is a sense of formality that flatters the people you are briefing. They are worth calling a proper meeting for – you obviously felt it was important that they should know, and should have a chance to ask for clarification if they need it.

You need to communicate all the information that people will want to know about this decision:

- ▶ **what the decision is**
- ▶ **who it will affect**
- ▶ **when it will happen**
- ▶ **what changes to expect**
- ▶ **how and by whom the decision will be implemented**
- ▶ **why you have arrived at this decision.**

That's all pretty straightforward, apart from the last bit: explain why you've chosen this option. If you've gone for the option everyone wanted, you may not have much trouble with this. But suppose you *are* making everyone wear uniforms? Or banning all overtime? Or moving accounts into an even grottier office than the one they're in now?

You've got to sell this decision to everyone. Show them why it's the right one. Persuade them that, in your position, they would have reached the same conclusion. To do this you need to:

- ▶ **Outline the key arguments in favour of the decision.**
- ▶ **Present the decision in a way that emphasises any benefits to them ('We'll provide the uniforms, so you no longer have to buy yourselves clothes to wear to work ...').**

QUESTIONS NOT CHALLENGES

You need to give people an opportunity to question you for clarification and understanding, but make sure you don't get into a slanging match, or let people think they can persuade you to change your mind. So allow reasonable questions, but make it clear that this is not the forum for arguing the toss. If you allow people to challenge your decision you will undermine your own authority, and give the impression that there's a chance they might overturn the decision. In fact the decision is made, it is the best decision, and you are committed to it. Make this clear for everyone's sake.

- ▶ Explain the key reasons why this option didn't come up to scratch if everyone favoured another option you rejected. Most people will submit to rational argument, however reluctantly.

- ▶ Show you took their views into account. Remember you took notes when you consulted? Well, now's the time to use them: 'Most of you in accounts told me that improved storage was your top priority, and you have that in the sub-basement.' 'Sarah pointed out to me that your clothes often get marked and damaged by the machines. You won't have to worry about that any longer.' (But don't make it sound as if it's all Sarah's fault they have to wear uniforms from now on.)

You have to become a salesperson for the duration of the briefing session, and be prepared to sell the decision to your colleagues and staff just as you would sell your products or services to a customer.

CONFIRM IT IN WRITING

Finally, once you have finished the session, reiterate the main points in a written memo. Not only does this add weight and finality to your decision, but it also ensures that everyone continues to have the same version of events. The grapevine withers and dies in the face of written communications. They leave no room for doubt or speculation.

In your memo, restate the points listed above reminding people what the decision is, how, when and by whom it will be implemented, and what to expect as a result of it. After going through this communication process, you should find that you have the support and the commitment – or at least the consent – of everyone you need, and hopefully their enthusiasm as well.

You need to communicate all the information that people will want to know

On this occasion, you have been so pushed for time that you have no option but to pass on your decision as soon as you've made it. In future, however, when you'll have more time (of course you will), it can be wise to wait a day or two before imparting your decision. The reason for this is that it helps you get it straight in your own mind, and allows time for any deep-seated, barely conscious niggles to come to the fore. If there is a nagging doubt in the back of your mind, you need to address it – perhaps even change your mind if you realise you'd missed something vital.

Nineteen times out of twenty, you won't even consider changing your mind. But a break between deciding and communicating the decision still doesn't hurt. It gives you a couple of days to feel really committed to it.

If you do give yourself the luxury of a break before you impart your decision, however, for goodness sake keep it to yourself. Otherwise the rumour-mongers will have time to start up, if anyone gets wind of what you're about to announce. And even if you put everyone straight within a day or so, they will still feel put out that they weren't the first to hear.

Decision making is always easier without the clock ticking, even if you're not going to waste time over it. The best approach is to do it fast (but not too fast), do it smart, and do it without pressure. That way you'll be effective, confident, and you'll join the ranks of the great decision makers.

The grapevine withers and dies in the face of written communications

decision in an evening

So, you've got to make an overnight decision. You've got this evening (or perhaps you have a morning or an afternoon) and then the decision has to be made. People are waiting for you. There's a temptation to panic, and to come out with any decision just to meet the deadline. But deep down you know that if it's the wrong one, it'll be worse in the long run than no decision at all. But you simply don't know which option to choose.

Don't panic. By the end of the evening you'll have a decision, you'll be confident it's the right one, and you'll be ready to defend it if you need to. Just follow the guidelines in this book, and speed it all up a bit:

- **Set your objective properly at the start. It won't take a moment, and it will ensure that you stay on track. This isn't the place to cut corners.**

- **Make sure you have to take this decision at all. Are you sure it isn't someone else's decision really? Or that it isn't**

dependent on another decision? If you don't need to take it now, you could have this evening off – so don't launch into the process until you're sure you have to.

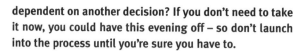 Give yourself a strict time limit for assembling the facts – about an hour and a half. Decide which are the 'must know' facts (see pages 12 to 14), and just stick to these.

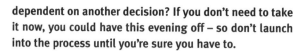 Ignore all the bumf on the subject in your file (you've got a file on this, I trust?), unless it happens to be on your 'must know' list. If it's not, it's simply a distraction.

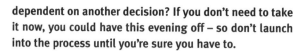 Make any phone calls to collect information first, before you look elsewhere for it; it can be hard to get hold of people at short notice and you don't want to miss them.

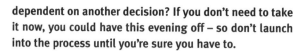 if you're collecting facts on the phone from someone you also need to consult, do this at the same time. Don't call them back again in an hour.

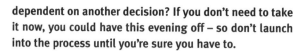 You'll have to do your consulting over the phone (unless you're in the office and the person you want to speak to is right next door). Keep your consultations short, but ask people what their preferred course would be and why. At least they'll feel they've been included in the decision.

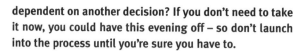 Write down your options, and if you feel you may be missing something, try one of the creative thinking techniques on pages 34 to 40 to help generate more. They don't take long, and if the right decision isn't down on your list somewhere, you'll have no chance of choosing it.

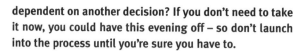 The right decision may be jumping out of the list at you. But if it isn't, do a risk/reward evaluation for each option (see pages 43 to 48). Eliminate as many options as possible this way.

By the end of the evening you'll have a decision, you'll be confident it's the right one, and you'll be ready to defend it if you need to

- ▶ If you're still uncertain, slim down your options using the 'Can I sleep at night?' process (pages 54 ot 55) – it's the quickest.

- ▶ You should be there now – the decision should be clear. If it's so close you really can't decide, and you're running out of time, just toss a coin. Go on. But whatever side it comes down on, commit yourself to that decision.

If it's so close you really can't decide, just toss a coin

decision in an hour

Wow! You like to live dangerously. I can only assume, if you've cut the decision this fine, that you've done most of your homework already. If this is a really important decision and you haven't even started assembling the facts, you're in big trouble. Bigger, in fact, than deferring the decision. So the logical thing to do is to delay the decision, no matter what hits the fan. It's still got to be better than making the wrong decision.

But let's suppose that you have assembled your facts. Maybe they've been sitting on your desk for weeks but you've been putting off the decision because the facts don't seem to be helping. In that case, we've still got time to tango.

1 Set your objective (pages 2 ot 4). Yep, sounds a waste of time, I know. But it's quicker than arguing, so just do it.

2 I imagine you've consulted already. I hope you've consulted. If not, pick the three or four key people who will be affected – or whose departments will be affected – by your decision, and speak to them. Ask them what they would like to happen and why. Keep the conversations brief – but make it very clear you're listening and you're really keen to know what they think. Feed this information into the decision.

3 Write down your options. Decide whether you reckon you've covered everything or if there may be another option you've missed.

4 If you need more options, use the problem reversal technique (pages 35 to 37) – it's quick and highly productive.

5 Now it's down to a process of elimination. Any option that clearly isn't the best can go – even if it's not bad. As soon as you can see any other option is better, the less good option gets struck off. So get rid of any options you can.

6 Now do a risk/reward evaluation on the remaining options (see pages 43 to 48).

7 Time's running out, so knock any other options on the head that you feel you can.

Any option that clearly isn't the best can go – even if it's not bad

8 If you have time, do the 'Can I sleep at night?' techinque (pages 54 to 55) on the remaining options.

9 Now decide. If it's completely impossible to choose between what's left, just toss a coin. Any option that's still left has got to be a reasonable decision at least. And taking the decision is probably more important than which of these you actually plump for.

Well done! You've reached the end of the beginning: the decision. Now all you have to do is communicate it and implement it. But if you've decided wisely, it should all be plain sailing from here.

Well done! You've reached the end of the beginning: the decision